A Winter on Earth

A Winter on Earth

Poems

Joseph Enzweiler

Iris Press
Oak Ridge, Tennessee

Copyright © 2006 by Joseph Enzweiler

All rights reserved. No portion of this book may be reproduced in any form or by any means, including electronic storage and retrieval systems, without explicit, prior written permission of the publisher, except for brief passages excerpted for review and critical purposes.

All photographs copyright © 2006 by Joseph Enzweiler

ACKNOWLEDGMENTS

Ice-Floe (Winter 2003): "Autumn Leaf" and "The Walk Home"
Ice-Floe (Summer 2004): "First Snow" and "Hurry Now"
Ice-Floe (Winter 2004): "Slop Bucket"
Ice-Floe (Summer 2005): "First Snow" and "First Rain"
Cream City Review (Winter 2005): "Christmas Tree"

Design by Robert B. Cumming, Jr.

Library of Congress Cataloging-in-Publication Data

Enzweiler, Joseph A.
A winter on Earth : poems / Joseph Enzweiler.
   p. cm.
ISBN-13: 978-0-916078-96-6 (alk. paper)
ISBN-13: 978-0-916078-97-3 (pbk. : alk. paper)
1. Winter—Alaska—Poetry. I. Title.
PS3555.N98W56 2006
811'.54—dc22
                                        2006027586

*With gratitude
for this life
in the North
and to all who
have shared it
with me.*

Contents

First Snow   13

I   SEPTEMBER

Traveler   17
Thompson Pass   18
Pine Grosbeak   19
Closing Up   20
Autumn Leaf   21
Late Blueberries   22
A Gift   23
Quiet   24
The Walk Home   25
Ruins of Day   26

II   OCTOBER

Dishes   29
So Much   30
Wood Splitting   31
For Jenna   32
Woodshed   33
College Corner   34
Let Us Walk Now   35
Dalton Trail   36

III   NOVEMBER

Kettle   39
Last Light   40
Little Bird   41
In Sorrow   42
Claw-footed Tub   43

Neighbors 44
Someone Walked This Way 45
On White 46

IV December

As Darkness Comes 49
Solstice 50
Duty 51
Remains 52
Pepper the Dog 53
A Thousand Years 54
Bed 55
Lydia / Signs 56

V January

The Wind 59
Heart of Cold 60
Christmas Tree 61
Great Ocean 62
Wood Stove 63
Sweet Light 64
The Performance 65
Static 66
First Sun 67
Sunburnt 68

VI February

Hour Before Dawn 71
Clamor of Sun 72
Slop Bucket 73
The World is Dressed 74
Shadows / Flicker 75
Winter Rooms 76

For Iris 77
Disappearing 78

VII March

Clearing 81
Apartment 82
The Way of Things 83
Musketeers 84
Cabin Door 85
Dream 87
Plague the Cat 88
Outhouse 89
The World is Speaking 90

VIII April

To You 93
History 94
Hurry Now / Stories 95
Guests 96
Mead 97
The Burden 98
Thirty Years / Time 99
Easter Night 100
Mud 101
Passageway 102

Afterword

First Rain 107

And we come back, the signs of time upon us,
In the pause of fate, the threading of the year.

—Kenneth Rexroth,
from "We Come Back"

First Snow

As on a journey to a place
you'll never reach, where love
waits in a distant face, days
of forest fall behind you,
then days of prairie.

But it always comes,
you're there as if foretold
and those miles blow away
on the winds of greeting.
Yet the thunderstorm remains,

violently blessing an evening
field, and the wrist of a girl
so thin as she poured coffee
one roadside evening, her face
(but you've forgotten)

was surely durable and good.
Summer holds us in its
never ending; grass in the wind
plays a yellow note. But now
the stove is lit. Ice turns

the strawflowers down. In kitchen
light, that face you traveled
years for. Let this never change,
you whisper to the porch at dusk.
Just then, it begins to snow.

I

September

Traveler

A last wild rose opens
in the roadside's slanted shade.

Soon hard frost melts
the contradiction of its red away.

Only the passerby who
in a yellowing world

answers hate with beauty,
though he is still undone,

knows why heaven uncloses its fist
in the white claws of the sun.

Thompson Pass

In the photograph, she kneels in lichen, in quilted pants along a shelf of granite. The sun is setting. Out of the frame, the west face of Mt. Blackburn glows with orange light. The blue hood of her windbreaker is tied at her chin, knees stained, face stung with cold and ready for home.

Ten thousand years harebell has grown here, alongside this rock, blue trumpets quivering on the stem. Soon we'll be gone and warm, this place forgetting us for the wild, stone-shaped wind. She offers to the camera cranberries, dark red, cupped in both hands. A smile struggles through the cold. The only things she can give now, the parting work of love.

Pine Grosbeak

Orange wings
at first
vanish into
autumn ground,

the way earth
someday will
possess him
that now
is the cloak
of freedom.

Though he sees me,
but plucks
a berry
like a king.

Such hiddenness
in certainty,
such knife blue
overhead,

each leaf
a question
set free from
its yellow stem.

Closing Up

Things left to do: finish the hole, jack the outhouse up and skid it over top; block up wheelbarrows with cedar planks; collect the cut wood before it snows. Screws in jars, tools on nails.

One morning you wake and it snowed all night. If you die this winter, friends in spring will find the last few tasks you cared about ascending through the snow. One more day, it would have been done. One more day.

It never comes, because *you* are the work, and joy is to dare the heavy gray sky, and despite the latest forecast, start in on something new.

Autumn Leaf

A blush of color
in the wind.
Everyone who
ever lived
was one.

What to say
of humankind,
under snow
and the sky's
cold justice,

but above,
blueberries
the birds
get drunk on
hang untaken,

tremulous
and sweet
on the stem.

Late Blueberries

Late autumn in the Goldstream Valley, the fresh snow softens in the sun. Beside the old railroad grade, blueberries still hang on leafless stems, frozen last night, now melting to droplets of blue, the heavy sweetness pulling at the berry's skin. I pick them gently as I can but they turn to liquid at my touch, cold fingers streaming blue, staining the hard white ground. No jar. No way to save what's here. I eat all I have and lick my hands, then home in the sharp winter light.

A Gift

All is as it should be,
supper finished, the rain
is over, clearing to the west.
A boreal owl, too young
to be afraid, glides
to a branch before me.

As it is at evening
this time of year,
when the woods hunt
tree to tree, I tried
to imitate its call,
a trill to bring it closer.

The little owl blinked
and gazed at me,
a wild incomprehension,
its answer, gliding off,
a burst of raindrops
on yellow leaves.

Quiet

Across the wheel barrow's pool of rain, a fallen leaf starts its journey. Down to 36° at night, the sandhill cranes are flying, fireweed turns to smoke and the rose hips redden.

Evening sun streams in the cabin, brilliant across the white gas stove and dusty picture frames, long shadows of spoons on the table, quiet as a photograph of the past. On the pine floorboards leaf shadows stir, silent hands of all who ever lived, retelling their stories in the wind.

The Walk Home

At the roadside,
cold grass
urgent
in the sun.

Friend,
once
we were close.

Now
a wind chime
sways
on the distant porch

of a neighbor
gone
for the year.

Ruins of Day

Each day is a water clock the ancient emperor builds. Chickadees at the feeder are its wooden cogs, turning the hours, a dynasty measured by black seed falling from birds choired in the spruce.

Night is the emperor's death, the clock torn apart by tomorrow, the new man. Time itself begins over with him by decree, his obedient court building on the ruins. Night and day, fast-hearted birds and the schemes of man, beneath a fierce indifferent blue.

II

October

Dishes

Melt snow, heat water
on the stove. A pan
for soap, one for rinse.

Put music on, let
the worst pots soak.
Try to tango with the cat.

For God's sake, after
thirty years, what *are*
you doing, you ask

one corner of the house,
this handmade box of life.
A favorite song comes on.

Pour a brandy,
the scrubbing pad
does a dance with plates.

The evening's almost brave.
Wrong number when
the telephone rings.

Black wind polishes
the sky. Another brandy,
maybe two. Ordinary things

while the dishes dry.

So Much

Clearing land to the east of alder and willow, so when summer comes, wild rose and horsetail will take hold, I cut a tall thin birch, bowed nearly to the ground. It would not have come back. With a crack it thuds in deep snow, is limbed and cut in sections, the brush hauled off. All that remains is the tree's impression, scattered hard leaves and a small black spider on the whiteness, frozen and perfect, shaken from a branch.

So much depends on a man with a saw, when he stops and what he chooses, what he bends to see. I stay a long time, hunched in the cold. "And you, tell me *your* history," I hear, as the sky bends down to me.

Wood Splitting

Balanced
on snow

arms raise
the ten pound

steel wedge
overhead

drive it down
through the handle's

curve of ash
in one high arc

shoulders and wrists
conspiring in the blow

two halves
of a man

gathered in
a single deed

and the alder splits
red with sweetness

For Jenna

The paper bracelet on her wrist never held this evening road, the sun by degrees narrowed to a bead in the poplars. In a mile I'll be at Susan's house, and a slow good meal. There's Venus over the airfield's unbroken white, the yellow west bending into black.

This sky is for Jenna, a face on a scrap of paper I found, who died at five weeks and left us here with the rugged work of the world. I think of her now, a hooded thought and half a mile to go, one note from a bow, she who never had evening.

Woodshed

Here's to the alder
I cut each day
down a winter trail,
carried home
shoulder high
fifty pounds
at a time,

like the troubled
heart I went at
with a sharpened saw,
so by day's end,
limbed and cut
in pieces like my thoughts,
I'd find
a wider clearing.

Now here it is
two winters on,
dry and three cords
square, carried
day by day inside,
undoing the past
in fire.

By spring, no trace
of all it held.
Even sorrow yields
its warmth.
The shed floor's swept,
I'll move my bed
and desk out there
by May, put on
a clear roof
for the sun.

College Corner

A young man turns the corner. Snow slants in a street light. In a heavy coat, he's come from a far place. I could run and ask his name. I do not. It was thirty years ago.

Another snow falls in the same light. A young man walks there, boots and a pack, toward the darkness across the railroad tracks. I could hurry and learn his name. I do not, and he is gone.

Who on earth is not the walker, a shape you may have known? Who is not the one who let him go? And always there is the street, the years, the slanted light, the snow.

Let Us Walk Now

No need
to speak.

We've known
each other
many years.

Listen
to the wind,

how the woods
move
with a
single mind.

Dalton Trail

The wind talks under my hat. A dog is barking. Down the road headlights stop and check the mail. I never look to see who wrote me until I'm home, a mile walk up the road, a little game to lengthen the mystery. Two days from full, the pale moon brightens in the birches. The dog is quiet. A star appears, then a hundred. To the south, Fairbanks glimmers with the weight of life. I turn off the road and through the woods, crossing bars of shadow down the path toward home, just me and whoever wrote today, right here in my coat pocket.

III

November

Kettle

The house is still.
One lamp is on,
serving spoons
upright in a jar.

You are so young
in the photograph,
girl with a violin
in summer shoes.

My rocking chair
stops like an
unwound clock.
Night comes early now,

a year already
since you married.
Nothing in the world
is moving,

basket of old clothes
in the corner, leaves
under snow, books
whispering from a shelf.

Then the kettle moans
like a faraway train.
Life in November's
bare lit hours

and a cup of tea
with lemon.

Last Light

By November, the sun never rises above the hill. Gone are the filaments of light on the cabin logs. Only the tallest spruce are lit for an hour, their dark green touched with rose, like sorrow burning in the mantles of great lamps.

I head home, on one shoulder wood for the stove. The path disappears behind me. God, it is winter again. It seems no time at all since I was young. All the days of my life could be like this, bits of the sky, violet forested nights. In a gap through the trees, there's Deneb in the Northern Cross, polished by the wind.

Little Bird

It matters much,
the little bird
that takes a seed,

who hurries out
and back all day,
who in her need

meets a shaft of sun
with cold regard,
as manic life

and sturdy death
bargain for her cloak.
That time is strife,

then time is gone
as you and I will be,
is neither happiness

nor grief. Violet
evening comes, and night
is one seed less.

In Sorrow

As the day grows dark, I put on a tape of Hildegard von Bingen, a soul shipwrecked on the rock of God. Her voice fills the cabin. I light a bottle candle in each window; they burn for a hundred hours.

Thanksgiving soon. I'll hear my friends laugh right here. They'll carry up the dark trail a casserole and trays of dessert. Work's over for the year. Tonight I'll take a bath.

From the porch, I see how summer stars drift west, night by night, on windless sails. And winter stars ascend—the Pleiades, Orion and Taurus over the power lines and my neighbor Jim's junk cars.

Inside a woman's voice searches the house, looking for happiness in sorrow.

Claw-footed Tub

How green the day was
when we brought the tub
home, rolled it on logs
up the path to the porch.

Mosquitoes were in bloom
as we sweated it there.
Wild rose opened out
like our minutes on earth.

I still see it stand
in the wavering shade
as I scrubbed the cast iron,
polished it black

and we had a home.
We sat in hot water,
two orchids unfolding
at the start of the world.

As if I'd been sleeping,
that's four summers ago.
She's in Florida now
and winter is here.

Like it is when we sleep,
the world makes no sense.
Time is as nothing
in the forest of dreams.

May the cold sun forgive
the sorrows that wake us.
I'll trade them a moment
tonight and be clean.

Neighbors

The moon drifts from a fire-blue cloud. The inverted V of Taurus glimmers above the transformer. The two stars of Orion's knees clear the snarls of alder, silent and choked with snow. The wind is beautiful and swift on the hilltop, yet still in these houses are the ordinary rooms where people live.

Someone Walked This Way

Someone walked this way,
peace or trouble measured
on a road, footsteps
tomorrow covers with a
quiet inch of snow.

Stars and cold are
the walkers now, wind
and sky. It does not matter
whose steps those were.
No one went by.

On White

Four inches of snow had fallen by morning. As far as one looks, the ground is untouched. But under a single birch, a million yellow seeds are scattered on the snow, a shudder sometime in the night.

IV

December

As Darkness Comes

Kneel a moment
on this winter path
where berries bleed
haloes in the snow.

Taste its fleck of red
melting in your palm.
Cold fingers, star
in the hastening clouds,

then a voice
"Remember me."
You turn, it is
no one, only the heart

patching a worn
and fragile cloth,
a face once loved
fallen to thread and time.

Walk forever and look
for heaven. Yet here
God's breath stains
your palm. The place

you seek is given.

Solstice

Even at noon, day remains a blue dust, the votive sun far south on the Alaska Range. Here on the north side, birds come and go, fast hungry silhouettes.

Laura knocks at my door, her dogs and sled tied to a birch. I'm happy she came. There are few visitors. "These are the days for seeing friends," she says. The pot of tea is a fire between us. The dogs grow quiet; they dig places in the snow.

We have an hour, then the busy coats and boots again, dogs straining at their lines. Day goes fast; shadows weave the trees together. She unties the sled and lifts the ice hook, and with a hand raised back to me, glides into evening. Inside, in the red chair, a trace of where she sat, and a little tea left in the cup. The pot still warm.

Duty

Here's a poem
to the hour
before dawn

one candle
forgotten
on the sill

all night
flickering
in its glass

as often
men and women
live their lives

no one sees
as they wave
to the dark

and warm
one panel
of the world

Remains

He sleeps downstairs beside the furnace and the blue fixed star of its pilot light, and many nights goes out late to meet her, turning the quiet skeleton key, across the cool dark lawn, rehearsing for a life to come.

Longing becomes routine, the graveyard shift, an hour at a table, bottled beer for a prop. As winter yields to April, everything between them has been said; they grow silent together in a corner as on a long journey, familiar pieces of each other glimpsed through noise.

He goes home with her, that's what remains, his arm over the shoulders of her white jacket, her hair a fall of black water. He never sees the sorrow in the corners of her moments.

Across the street in the brick alleys between shops, Ailanthus trees reached toward the light. He believes he loves her, and the streets glisten with rain.

Pepper the Dog

Loyalty,
that so many years
kept pace beside
his striding thoughts,
when he turns to look,
is gone.

It's he who must
be loyal now,
calling as he goes
her memory
from snow
and starry woods.

Many nights
you see them
out walking the ridge,
a man in a coat,
an old dog
unforsaken
at his heel,
in a beloved
gust of wind.

A Thousand Years

The quietest place in the world is under a spruce tree in the heart of December. Snow weighs the branches down to a tent of shadow. One thread of sun slips in at mid-day, like eyes opened from sleep, uncomprehending.

Only a redpoll marks the seconds, clinging a moment to the bark, taking a seed. A candle lit here would still burn after ten thousand years, in thick green glass.

Or is the quietest place when someone is there, listening? Or when someone far away imagines himself there, listening to that imagined place?

Bed

Frame of pine,
old mattress, pillow
leaking feathers
at the seams.

Then morning is given,
the little boat
of the soul is home.
A chair and coffee,

a tiny moth hatching
from window dust,
its wings a candelabra,
a dream.

Last night the stars
shone bright as apples,
today the sky
is bladed wind.

Joined and true
is our frame of earth,
leaking its heaven
all the days we wake.

Lydia

The setting sun starts fires in the shed windows. Cirrus clouds curl on the great shear winds from Asia. This sky is for Lydia, how her face moved one winter afternoon as fifteen candles on the tree were lit, as though in her eyes the quiet woods flew with a hundred birds, hungry and flecked with color, startled by something beyond hearing, many years ago.

Signs

Breast feathers from a grouse scatter across the road, soft as smoke onto night's fresh snow. Twenty feet away lay a dark form, broken and moving in the wind. Overhead scalloped clouds on the last day of December drift west, slowly over the power lines.

V

January

The Wind

Night of the full moon.
Orthodox Christmas.

Birch trees creak
like antique chairs,

snow thudding at the porch
as the cat's eyes widen.

Let's walk tonight
while the road drifts closed,

where the city
glitters from the hill,

our thoughts
torn from us

as the wind burns
past our hoods.

Heart of Cold

Where it runs through the wall, I grip the plastic pipe that drains my tub. It cracks with my hand's warmth. One more bath and it would be solid ice. Nail heads in the door are globed with frost. When I open it, the cat's thrown back by a slab of minus 40.

Last night the propane stopped, so it's breakfast on the wood stove. A roof rafter popped at four in the morning and woke me. The only moving thing in the house tonight is the steel flap squeaking on its bead chain, as the cast iron stove draws air.

Christmas Tree

January tenth, twilight
lingers long past four.
Loosened from its stand,
raining needles, I carry it
back into the cold, across
the bridge and thrust it
upright in the snow.
The same newspaper
that caught the candle wax
sets the tree ablaze.

How briefly that flame
rules the evening field.
When I look back,
a few embers on a reach
of white, the way
our own days close
their furrowed hours
behind us, and that
was life, a little boat
on the phosphorus sea.

Great Ocean

East on Beechmont Avenue, the eyes of the brick houses are all shut. Factory smoke twists over leafless ash and locust as a three-quarter moon comes up. When they arrive, on the building's dark façade, her doorbell is lit.

Today no road goes there, no number rings in the silent kitchen, no telephone book with the lover's names. Their breath turns to ice on the windshield. She is crying, homesick for Japan. When she was a girl, she tells him, a rabbit made rice cakes on the moon.

From the parking lot as far as they can see, the high grass moves like an ocean. Nowhere to go from here. They have driven to the edge of the world.

Wood Stove

Cast in fire,
now holding fire,
your life has been
one thing. Tell
these hands you love them
one more arctic night.

The gloves are dry
and soup is hot
like a day of wages.
Half a life I worked for you,
bringing wood all those
homeward afternoons.

You're just a tended
iron thing, and love's
not the kind of fire
you hold. Yet there is debt
I cannot name. I stand
palms down before you

as in prayer to the creator:
there is only warmth
and only cold.
Here before you, keep me
from the headless night.

Sweet Light

Now is the time of sweet light. The sun's work is done. Wildfire smears the window glass. The birch tops are tapers of purple-gold like objects used in worship. From a thicket far below, one heavy clump of snow falls; the branch, remembering, breathes up and comes to rest. Nothing moves again all night. How slow the spring is coming.

The Performance

Where is my silk shirt now, with a razor's
dot of blood I folded to never wear again,
that plywood clock with fat white hands
we nailed together and slid out on the ice,
whose mouth the little frogs skated through
and made the building smile?

All the untutored kind applause the bleachers
poured down upon our dance,
or where that man and woman went
who looked like us in the overhead
mirrored tiles, señor and señorita?
Winter cars in the parking lot, things
the girders whispered after the rigging
and colored lights were struck?

Or the rose you pinned that Sunday
to my lapel in the curtain's slit of light,
one of twelve I gave you
and there we were, wet in the eyes,
as if all the cold rehearsals touched
now and then with victory, grew
nearly big enough to say?

The music cued us and we disappeared.
The little frogs grew up. We danced
the tango just as planned, then hauled
the clock off in my truck.
Only the rose remains, on my wall
above the stove, a bloom of dust
as the girders wait for the lights to dim,
the music plays so red, and we are young.

Static

Years ago, Sunday night listening to the radio. A woman speaks in Yupik, speaks of salvation, her voice urgent and soft, to anyone out there in the darkness. When she finishes, a man comes on in English. It is two in the morning, snow falling on the empty streets of Fairbanks.

"This concludes our broadcasting day. KUAC is rebroadcast on the following transmitters: in Nenana on K216AN at 91.1 megahertz; in Healy on K269AD at 101.7 megahertz; in Central, Circle & Circle Hot Springs on K219AD at 91.7 megahertz…"

His voice is calm. Yes, tomorrow I can listen again, that voice will fill my truck heading home, when days are short and the orange drop of the sun falls early behind the mountains.

"Good Night," he says, and the Alaska State Flag song comes on, women's voices trailing off…"the simple flag of the Last Frontier." Then static. All across the dial there is only the hiss, the long night, snow falling as far as the mind can reach.

Years ago, when town could be quiet a little while and a wilderness play its hush on the radio till dawn. In me too, a wilderness, the future still a wide imagined thing, new in my house and heading home, two sawhorses for a kitchen, happy that I was warm.

First Sun

Tendril waving
on the cabin wall,
first sun in ten weeks,
an infant's eyes
fluttering in her crib.
How long were we shadows,

my friends and I,
though we laughed and ate
under the blue stone
of December?
Stay a second longer

on the nail heads,
once dulled with ice,
now fierce iron stars.
And come tomorrow
a little higher
through that notch of trees.

I'll be here,
a hammer echoing
in the heart, how I
lived to build
this house another year.

Sunburnt

She watches him put the shirt on, the one she bought, a blue simple gift. She straightens its newness away like crumbs. What she feels for him presses in her face so evenly, it might hold a cup of rain.

He takes her hand, her fingers curling into a wren. At night, they kneel on the carpet in waterfalls of laughing, laborers sunburnt in summer wheat. When they stand at the window, the city takes off its clothes.

In sleep, her hair tangles in a parking light that slants through venetian blinds. They turn together, handholds in a dream of falling.

But today he wants a photograph, a faded scrap will do, anything so she could look at him again. For he can't recall her face.

VI

February

Hour Before Dawn

Shadow
of Venus
this moonless hour
when only
the bread truck
makes its rounds.

Though the years
are burned up
thin as paper,
your black hair
is quilted over us yet
that joy shook
into threads.

O World,
what we ask
of you
in the hour
before dawn,
when the bread truck
makes its rounds.

Clamor of Sun

February 1. The road facing north is a gray shadow. Tracks of a jet plane are etched on blue. As I near the top the snow is burning, a clamor of light on the metal shed. Telephone wires are incandescent as though I was missing a great event down here in my north-facing shade. The sun burns my face. Its light is cold and the wind is cold. There has not been a cloud in ten days, not a breath of wind. Go get the mail. Wave to someone passing, lost in a coat as I am. Tonight a crescent moon. Every road is holy.

Slop Bucket

Before you went to a blessed rest
with a leak sprung from sheer fatigue,
you held toothpaste and sour milk,
taco meat with blue-green fuzz,
grease and old coffee. It was
your calling, like the poor souls
in Purgatory, to hold awhile
these things I did and who I was—
only moments ago regarded kindly—
now a swirl of dark indignities.

You lived to be twenty, a hundred
in people years. I thank you now
for all you gave so I could spit,
be sick, even pee on winter days
when I couldn't face the door.
In the gulley I pour you out
a final time, tired and slick inside,
as Dante might have done if he lived here.

Then for a second a little bird
February killed is floated up and thawed,
a useless clotted thing. But its wing
catches the day's last bit of sun,
gleaming so blue I fall in love:
with an old bucket like a friend.
Life with its farewells.
The suddenness of heaven.
The utility of hell.

The World Is Dressed

They have breakfast from stainless trays, bacon and scrambled eggs, night still stirring in their eyes and hair. She goes with him for a little while. His young face lifts her from a marriage that has become a door key and a few taped boxes.

Among the echoes of commerce and blur of human voices, they are happy in their small devotions, their fingers and hips touch with knowledge, their footsteps going easy on a morning without clocks, the bargain with Eden covered by unironed clothes.

Shadows

Sun's
hour hand
on the snow.

Two black
coats are

but seconds
passing.

Flicker

In quiet
snowy woods:

tut, tut, tut

one small
busy head.

Winter Rooms

The woods are alive. The full moon on the 23rd pours shadows all night across the snow, setting pale at dawn over the west hill. Time of resurrection as the sun seeps back in these winter rooms.

Today a drip began inside. A little glacier loosens one shingle till water, that thief, picks the lock and slips in. Half-asleep, I stumble into the cold, night's warmth seeping away, in my parka and untied boots. I shovel and bang the ice away, come in for coffee, go back to bed and listen.

When I wake, the sun is so high I clean six window panes facing south above the tub, feel its strength for the first time since September.

Twenty years ago I put that window in, mitering the frame, scored and snapped each pane of glass to fit, then glaze and paint. The sun was exactly as it is today, though I dreamed of other things back then, when I was thinner and so full of plans in my red untrimmed beard.

For Iris

Just a little thing for you
on the day you were born,
one finch landing on my porch,
plunged to the breast
in morning's inch of snow,
head cocked up at me,
two black specks as if amazed
that yesterday is gone.

Then the first seed falls
on a white new world
from others clattering
in the spruce above.
Soon all becomes as it was before,
ground strewn with sunflowers
cracked for the heart's warm oil.

If I could, I'd give you
for your crib, daybreak's
blue cloth, and a bird
like this one for your tiny fist,
you unclose tomorrow into all
that's tremulous and good.

Disappearing

A thin rain burned to blue by ten. They never knew, walking in the sun down the black reflecting tiles as morning yawned with pleasure, that they were already the past. I watch them by the row of shops, demolished long ago and built upon, past the fountain water gliding on parabolas of wire, past Newmark's record store and windows of sweaters on headless bodies, the aroma of face cream yielding to lemon tea. He kisses her on the hair, she leans her thoughts into his shoulder, their talk a few bits of cloth sent toward the wind. How far away they are beneath the skylight. Five steps past the curio shop, each time I look, right there they turn to dust, his claim still on her lightly at the sleeve of her sweat shirt.

VII

March

Clearing

The deep March snow.
Birches slender in the earth,
birds from their sides
feed as they've done
for a thousand years.

I tell you this
as if I'd given you that place.
If we meet again,
take my hand.
I was wrong, I'll say,

a cup of words was all
I had, tipped over a little way.
But no regrets.
There's still a path
going there.
I can't describe it.
Together we'll go and see.

Apartment

Her place is like the others, the bedroom a mirror of the one next door, a common wall of pipes, heating ducts where the breath of strangers joins. The porcelain comes standard, stainless sink, a clean tan rug. Which one of them is hers, in that block of a hundred lives, surveyed years ago and graded over to an exit ramp with its furious knot of commerce.

Long ago they slept there, where today the rain slants through. Not the one beside it, but that room where I'm pointing, on the second floor paneled by the sky, with its hot bath water and pear-scented soap.

The Way Of Things

A woodpecker flies
in a thicket loud
with melting snow.

The thicket quivers,
a thousand droplets
fall. And the boy

who changed the world,
still watches, after
a lifetime, joy vanish

with a shudder,
while the bird
with a fiery crown

of feathers,
claims for itself,
the sun.

Musketeers

My three cats sit at the window like decanters. Shoulder to shoulder, they watch birds land and fly, their heads synchronized metronomes, tails of different lengths flailing away, ready for business.

Lady Padhorn swishes hers like Jackson Pollock, her inner canvas a swirl of headless themes. Bad to the Bone Jerome, his Japanese Bobtail four-inch brush flicking, parrying, a notable but lesser master as Little Man, the Manx, my artistically challenged son, twitches his nub like a mouse trapped in a sock. One must have dreams.

But today, they are all Michaelangelos, chickadees frescoed onto morning's Sistine Chapel, each in the first year of their long illustrious careers.

Cabin Door

Friend, mute thing
I shake hands with
every day, who for
twenty-five years
let me escape
in both directions,
I remember the night
of the Coleman lamps
when I was so young
the world was all
fiberglas and plywood,
my breath an apparition
in the block of cold
that would be home.

And you, too heavy
to lift, sledded here
by moonlight, shimmed
and bolted on, felt
around the edges to seal
out the rapier wind.
As if this was my
spaceship to the stars,
emissary in a corner chair
from a world that,
as I arrive in greeting
light years hence,
is no longer there.

You watched it all,
June's leafy sun, winter
loosening into sap and mud.
On the other side,

old loves of mine
and meals alone.
Till I stand up
one more time, put on
my coat and greet you.
Daylight floods in hinged
and white. Don't wait
for me. Can't promise
I'll be back, as you
repeat what my father
told me once, from your
deepening veneer:
"I hope you find
what you're looking for."

Dream

On wings
grown of muscle and blood
I carry you high
above winter.
We drink each other,
hunting the sorrowful
earth, happy
in the yellow
sacrament of the sun.

I wake
bleeding where the wings
have torn away.
It is Tuesday,
I never knew you.
Now it is *I*
who am the prey.

We are always
of two hearts.

Plague the Cat

All the books of poems I wrote, back when my beard was red, Sundays on the phone to Dad, alone in his small apartment, a breeze in the red maple outside the window counting his minutes, mornings of coffee and nights of wine—for twenty-one years she was there on my lap.

I made a box from old plywood stored beneath the cabin, cut the pieces on the porch. The first snow in weeks began falling, windless and silent as day faded. I hovered above grief, detached from the box that suddenly was finished, my hands moving in the old ways I've known all my life with wood, Plague the cat still warm in her red blanket on the deck beside me.

"I'll use the three-inch screws," I decided, the ones with Phillips heads I kept in a mason jar, until the silver screws became the last thing I could give, holding tight the wooden boat I'd send her off in. I laid her in there, ran power to the drill and said goodbye. For six days she was in the woodshed, the days still frozen, on a pile of hand-cut alder.

In the morning I went out along the stone wall and shoveled away three feet of snow, and with a mattock, began on the rock-hard ground.

Outhouse

Here's a magazine
wrinkled with movie stars,
their divorces last year's news.
A calendar from '92
with phases of the moon,
days recalled a second or two
like dusting a shelf
with thoughts: summer work,
the price of gas back then,
tea with a dying friend.

Above is a row of empty bottles,
the weddings of my friends.
There's Mark and Judy,
my brother Steve who's now
remarried, some labels forgetting
who they were, bleached by sun.
For them, the ocean *was* that day,
the sun champagne, now just
tapered glass devotions.

But churches are for praying
and this isn't a church exactly,
or one in spirit if not
in kind. Toilet paper's
in a can to keep out squirrels.
The wind is elegant and warm,
shifting a few lost leaves.
Joy too is the business
of the world, and ice
drips hotly from the eaves.

The World Is Speaking

Second day of big wind, the final week of March. The sun is fierce by day, temperature near zero. Caught in the shallows of the path, twigs and spruce comes, yellow seeds of birch, curled birch bark so thin the light comes through them rose-gold. An empty box tumbles across the porch.

For days, no one calls. Only a northeast wind and the day's clockwork shadows. Last night it blew at the house like a great beast. The moon is new, thin as a flake of ice. A blade of cold seeps around the window; the wood stove gulps. Go walking in a heavy coat. Cover your neck. The world is speaking urgently. Its words are scattered everywhere. Their meaning is the wind.

VIII

April

To You

who aren't yet born,
I give the brown sparrow
the size of my thumb

just now on a branch,
six leaves shuddering
in the western sun.

What they mean
I wondered too,
but already it's long ago.

Sparrow, green
seeds of sun.
Take them,

they are yours now.
You'll know
what to do.

History

A path goes to the outhouse over the wooden bridge, and one to where the slop bucket's dumped. Down to the truck, behind the cabin for firewood. In winter they pack hard as if they'd last forever; any good map would show them. There's history under the bird feeder, fallen seed pressed between snows, a geology the voles tunnel through.

My boots mutter along the trail as I listen in. Thoughts come and go, though I've forgotten now, worries punctuated by clouds of breath. Two thousand pounds of wood cut in winter's narrow light, that's my conclusion.

Then history softens in the sun. Where I walked is runoff now and cold black earth. Here's a photograph of those paths, only a month ago. That's what the world was like, a few ways of going. They're only where a man once walked, what he needed for a little while.

April is amnesia, a green Assumption. There's a soft hiss off new leaves, unlike autumn's sound of tin. The forest returns as it has always been, washed of the steps of man.

Hurry Now

Spring's
last snow
gone by noon.

Come,
some innocence
yet

on the world's
dark boughs.

Stories

Sun glints
off the green
wine bottle.

We two,
silent
on the porch.

Guests

Caribou simmers in sweet alder smoke. Black stones of clouds hang in the west. Light stays late this time of year, the anxious sun just below those hills and a green midnight sky. The hour slows as I put on music and set the table for one. A candle in its metal holder throws stars against the ceiling. Broccoli and wild rice are nearly ready, a paper towel folded under the fork. I dish up the meat from a black iron pan. Down the hill, cold melt water from the day bubbles under nighttime ice. A boreal owl trills for a mate. The planet Saturn is high in the east by 9. The clock stops as I sit down with the world and listen. I seldom eat alone.

Mead

Out the thin tubes
birch sap pours,
three hours to a gallon.
In only a day,

there's no place left
to keep it. I drink
what I can, cold
from metal pails.

Stars command night,
but late in March, sun
is master of the day.
Limbs click with wind

like a carriaged street
siphoned into blue
by thaw and desire.
Each night, one bottle

bursts, a gunshot
in the dark. What survives
till summer, opened
on the hottest days

escapes the way the soul
might go, into fizz
and sugared air, just an inch
remaining of a labor

hard on earth,
but tasting sweet.

The Burden

Islands of dark widen in the snow, clotted grass and horsetail from last September until what remains are islands of white, disappearing by the hour. In the middle of the night, a final slab of snow rumbles from the roof, two thousand pounds shuddering the walls, waking me, widening the cat's yellow eyes. For a second, it's the end of the world. Then something eases within, the house breathes up, unchained from winter. It happens this way every spring, the lifting of a burden that has no name.

Thirty Years

Her wrist,
persimmon.

The heart's
black earth
still grows

a tall
persimmon tree.

Time

Forever
we promised

in our
windy field

where a city
now stands.

Easter Night

The trees are hinged and creak in the starlight. A few leaves tick past, and wind makes snow devils at the corners of my house.

It takes six days to dig her grave. I make three fires a day in that square of frozen ground, get it roaring with an armload of wood, then shovel out the coals and thawed wet silt, gaining a few inches, then beginning again. I carry earth by bucketfuls inside the house, to keep it workable, pour them out on an old blue tarp in the middle of the floor.

"All right, let's do this," I tell my friend, and we carry the box out to the wall. It is Easter night, the time of year boreal owls begin to call. I light a kerosene lamp, slip a rope through the I-bolts in the lid to lower her softly as I could, as if to say "You'll be down there just a little way, in your silver-fastened boat, and I'll be right here."

The stars are sharp as voices tonight, and lamp light mutters on the snow. I slip the rope out and coil it on one arm, then haul the buckets of earth back out, two by two. I finish after midnight, sweating, take off my shirt by the wood stove. We stand there a long time, in silence, and have a glass of wine.

Mud

My truck whimpers
like a dog let out to pee,
which is actually only me
in love with spring.
But a hundred yards
up the road, a little
short of where I planned,
I'm up to the hubs
in April mud and my neighbor's
cigarette's flamboyant salute.

His father died this year.
Their '26 Dodge waits
in the yard. We stand
and talk around the facts,
then talk some more.
"I'll winch it out after
one more beer." Well, that's
just fine. Hand me one too.
Until Jim's just the tip
of his cigarette, the moon

sets, slim as a paring knife
and the muddy ruts glow
with jagged light. Leave
the damn thing! Tonight's
too good to be stuck someplace,
and getting there, wherever
it was, as we turn and wave
in the dark, was not
where we had to go.

Passageway

You should be happy. The door stands open, pouring with sun, the roof is soft and melting. Snow shouts with blue shadows. The road is a gleaming rutted mess. Out on the porch, winter's slow congestion loosens in your chest. You should be free.

But April is hard; it asks much. Brightness bangs at your face like a sheet of metal. Your legs feel the tonnage of life. While owls mate and birches slough in the wind, you're asleep upstairs. You want to die. And the earth does not care; you are only one passenger.

Then one evening when only a star or two is left in the long twilight, you look up. Out of nowhere, you are happy, like a whisper, stepping one more year out that dark door, and it is spring.

Afterword

First Rain

They stretch on, late winter days
as though you lived another life
in late September, when snow
first fell. You were happy then,

or was it sad? In any case,
an old friend died and one was born.
Strawflowers melted and the sullen
grass laid down. Three cords

of birch slipped to the sky
and left you warm. Bare-chested
on the porch now, too cold yet
to live, too bright to sleep.

Just a few more weeks, through
the time of suicide and raw
April weather. We made it,
you and I, dark days, catastrophes

held back another winter by some
fortunate gift of warmth.
What was sorrow, now passes
on this morning air so soft,

you could take up winter once again.
Back when you were happy,
or was it sad? Just then,
it begins to rain.

Joseph Enzweiler was born in Cincinnati in 1950. He has lived in Alaska, in a cabin north of Fairbanks, since 1975. He works seasonally as a carpenter and stone mason.

His other books include *Stonework of the Sky* (Graywolf Press), *A Curb in Eden* and *The Man Who Ordered Perch* (both by Iris Press).

About the Book

This book is typeset in Adobe Caslon. William Caslon released his first typefaces in 1722. Caslon's types were based on seventeenth-century Dutch old style designs, which were then used extensively in England. Because of their incredible practicality Caslon's designs met with instant success. Caslon's types became popular throughout Europe and the American colonies; printer Benjamin Franklin hardly used any other typeface. The first printings of the American Declaration of Independence and the Constitution were set in Caslon. For her Caslon revival, designer Carol Twombly studied specimen pages printed by William Caslon between 1734 and 1770.

*This book was printed
in the United States of America
on acid-free paper.*

Joseph Enzweiler took all the photographs used on the cover and in this book over a period of many years in and around Fairbanks, Alaska.

About the Book

This book is typeset in Adobe Caslon. William Caslon released his first typefaces in 1722. Caslon's types were based on seventeenth-century Dutch old style designs, which were then used extensively in England. Because of their incredible practicality Caslon's designs met with instant success. Caslon's types became popular throughout Europe and the American colonies; printer Benjamin Franklin hardly used any other typeface. The first printings of the American Declaration of Independence and the Constitution were set in Caslon. For her Caslon revival, designer Carol Twombly studied specimen pages printed by William Caslon between 1734 and 1770.

*This book was printed
in the United States of America
on acid-free paper.*

Joseph Enzweiler took all the photographs used on the cover and in this book over a period of many years in and around Fairbanks, Alaska.

www.ingramcontent.com/pod-product-compliance
Lightning Source LLC
LaVergne TN
LVHW091311080426
835510LV00007B/461